40 POEMS FOR T

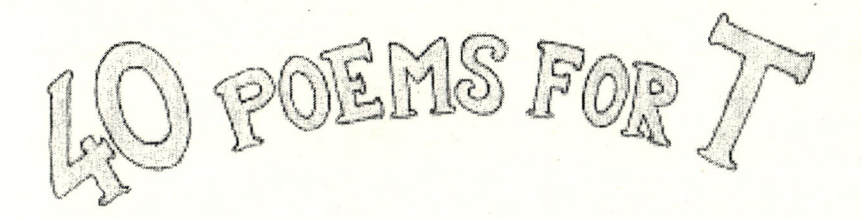

The fun of writing poetry

Press-TIGE Publishing

40 POEMS FOR T

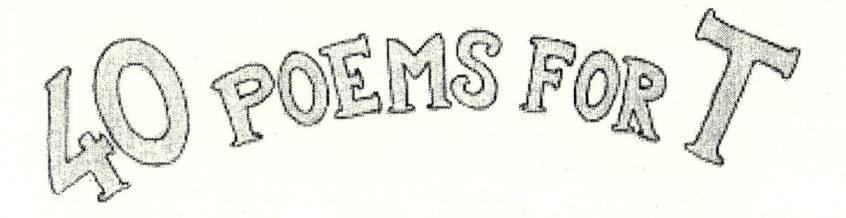

The fun of writing poetry

by
George L. Dyer, Jr.

Illustrated by Lena Kasten

Copyrighted 1999 by George L. Dyer, Jr.
Illustrations copyrighted 1999 by Lena Kasten
ISBN# 1-57532-287-0

All rights reserved. No part of this publication may be reproduced,
stored in a retrieval system, or transmitted
in any form or by any means—electronic, mechanical, photocopy,
recording or any other, except for brief quotations in printed reviews
—without prior permission of the publisher.

For information:

Press-TIGE Publishing
291 Main Street
Catskill, NY 12414
http://presstigebooks.com
Presstige9@aol.com

First Press-TIGE Edition 1999
Typesetting by: Drawing Board Studios

Printed in the United States of America

DEDICATION

This book is dedicated to Terrance "T" Adams. T is the 11 year-old son of George and Dobie's son's wife, Vicki. He works hard at his studies and is intensely curious about all things. He like sports, particularly football and soccer. He enjoys music and plays the clarinet. T is our friend, and we wish him the joy of words and the fun of writing poetry.

CONTENTS

Acknowledgments xi
Preface xiii
A Political Cat Called Clarence 3
Waiting for a Poem From Terrance 4
    What a *Poem* Is 6
    About *Ideas* for *Poems* 6
Ideas for a Poem 7
    A Game: *Acrostics* 9
Rats and Cats, Forever 9
    A Game: *Word Box* 10
Star Light 17
    About a *Journal* 18
    More About *Ideas* for *Poems* 18
    About an *Idea File* 18
A Short Poem 19
    About **Haiku** and **Senryu** and *Syllables* 19
Puget Sound Scenes ......
    Sunlight shining through 20
    In the thick, grey fog 20
    The South wind blowing 20
    Through glistening waters, ... 21
    In summer sun Blue 22
A Senryu
    "After you, Madam." 24
    About *Similes* and *Metaphors* 25
Haiku Metaphor 25
    About *Capital Letters* 27
Sunsets by T 29
Manta Rays by T 29
Wheels and Flies 30
Sharing 33
Getting the Word 34
Do You Drink Up or Down? 35

Flies Time	36
Snoring	38
Rings	40
The Empty Store	43
About *Rhymes*	44
About *Double Syllable Rhymes*	45
About *True Rhymes* and *Near Rhymes*	45
Please!	47
About *Stanzas*	48
A Game: *Football*	49
About *Alliteration*	52
The Reclus	52
More About *Football*	54
Whales! by T	55
About *Repetition*	56
A Saleman's Advice	57
Ephphie, the Ephelant	59
About *Limericks*	59
About *Meter*	60
The Mechanical-Minded Trojan	60
An Opera Diva Named d'Orso . . .	61
The Witch's Brew	62
Donut Holes	64
About *Internal Rhymes*	68
About *Scansion*	68
The Boy from Calcutta	70
The Man from Seattle	71
The Strange Man in Seattle	71
About *Titles*	72
Bugged by Matthew Dyer	74
About *Opening* and *Closing Lines*	74
Hypotenusey Lucy	77
A Bad Night for Trick or Treating by T	78
About *Point of View*	80
Oops Oops Soup . . .	81
A Game: *First Personing*	82
A Game: *Exquisite Corpses*	83
About *Poems in Special Shapes*	83
Catterpiggle	84

Milady Moon	85
About *Personification*	86
About Sonnets	87
The Personnetification of A Tree	88
About Free Verse	90
Sandpiper Tracks	90
More About *Metaphors*	92
A Game: *Getting More out of Your Metaphor*	93
For the Savor of Such a Moment	94
Black Ice	97
About *Imagery*	98
Advice	100
The Puddle at the Table	100
Words You Might Not Know	101
Bibliography	104

ACKNOWLEDGMENTS

We wish to thank the many people who helped us with this project, particularly the several educators who reviewed the manuscript as it developed: Sister Anne Dyer, the principal of The Stone Ridge School of the Sacred Heart, and Sister Karen Olson, one of her teachers; Mrs. Pat Nesbitt, a retired Vice Principal from California; Mrs. Mary Kay Panucci, a retired School District Superintendant from California, and H. James Jensen, Ph.D., Professor of English at Indiana University, since retired. Because of their excellent criticisms and suggestions, we revised the book substantially and added games to make it more accessible. Professor Jensen was enormously supportive. His encouragement was critical to keeping the project alive.

We also want to express our appreciation to the others that reviewed our work, including Jovi Monroe (an 11 year old educatee) and a young lady, whose name we do not have, that gave us valuable help at the Port Townsend Writer's Conference.

And finally, thanks beyond measure to George's wife Dobie Dyer, who puts up with his whimsey, creative urges and other distractions. Without her patient, good natured support, this book would have died long ago.

PREFACE

Dear T,

As you look through this book, you'll see that it is written in different styles of type. They're supposed to help you follow what we're talking about. The name of poems look like this:

Sharing

The poems themselves use the same type face, but not bold:

A political cat called Clarence,

The writing about the poems looks just like this paragraph. Particular kinds of poems are referred to in this same type, but bold face.

Haiku and Senryu

Finally, when we're talking about something that relates to poetry, the current topic is in italics, like this:

About a *Journal*

As I said, I hope it helps!

40 POEMS FOR T

2

Dear T,

Here's a poem for you. It'll be fun to share poems with each other.

A Political Cat Called Clarence

A political cat called Clarence,
Who was owned by a young lad named Terrance,
    On the stump said meows,
    While T waved and took bows,
Which won Clarence and Terrance adherents
Every time that they made an appearance.

So they went to the mice's convention,
Where they hoped for a lot of attention,
    And they really expected
    They would both be elected,
But there wasn't a single mouse delegate
Who would vote for a cat as a candidate.

Dear T,

Have you sent a poem? I haven't received one. Here's another for you, anyway.

Waiting for a Poem From Terrance

I thought that Terrance, my friend,
And I, from time to time,
Would to one another send
A poem, or at least a rhyme.

I sent him one based on his name,
But none has come back, you see.
I wonder what is to blame
For his failure to send one to me.

Can he not pick an idea
About which to write?
Can he not find a form
That pleases his sight?
Can he not think of words
That he feels are just right?

5

Dear T,

I'm really sorry if the last poem hurt your feelings. It wasn't supposed to do that. It was just supposed to let you know the questions to ask yourself in making a poem. You've asked what a poem really is and how to find an idea for a poem.

What a *Poem* Is

A *poem* is words written in a pattern. The words tell what you're thinking, what you feel. They do so in a stronger, more compact, more imaginative, and perhaps more beautiful way than everyday talk, even though they may sound like everyday talk.

A poet named Dylan Thomas had fun with poetry. He said, "*Poetry* is what makes me laugh or cry or yawn, what makes my toenails twinkle, what makes me want to do this or that or nothing. All that matters about *poetry* is the enjoyment of it..."

Another poet Robert Frost said, "*Poetry* is a fresh look and a fresh listen." He meant, what you, especially, see and hear.

And another, D. H. Lawrence, said "*Poetry* is a stringing together of words in a ripple and jingle and run of colors...an iridescent idea." That sounds like a Christmas tree, doesn't it?

About *Ideas* for Poems

If there are some words in this next poem that you don't know, you can look them up in the section at the back of this book called, **WORDS YOU MIGHT NOT KNOW**.

Ideas for a Poem

What's it take to make a poem?
Any idea that may come
Into your cranium,
Whether you're in your room
In your own home,
Or in Alaska at Nome,
Or under a dome
In a cathedral in Rome,
Or deep in a catacomb.
Now, I know that some
Say that a poem
Can only come from
The heart, but even a tome,
Or a Jeroboam,
Especially a Jeroboam,
Can provide the idea for a poem.

Many of the most fun *ideas* for poems come from words themselves and their sounds:

> lots of words with the same rhyme, like **Ideas for a Poem** that you've just read;
>
> puns, that is, words that sound the same but have different meanings;
>
> words and sayings that are funny if you twist them around;
>
> even riddles, as you'll see.

You can get *ideas* for poems from word games, too. Try these games and see if they give you some *ideas*.

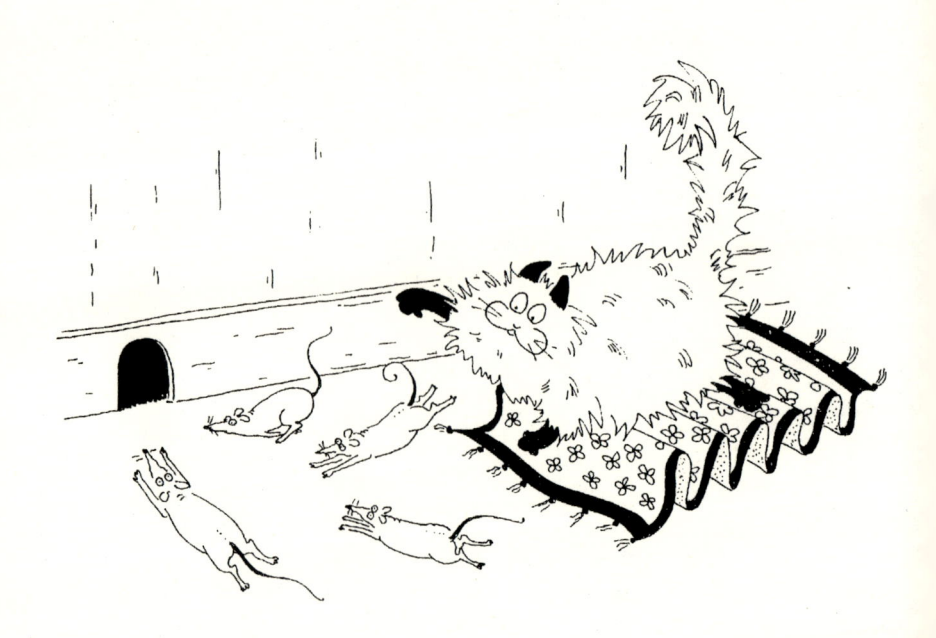

A Game: *Acrostics*

If you want to have some fun with words that might give you an idea for a poem, here's a good game. Take a word, any word. Write it down, up and down, on the left side of a page, so that each letter is the first letter of a different line. Then see if you can think of words that start with the letter at the beginning of each line and relate to the up-and-down word. Here's a sample.

Rats and Cats, Forever

Run
Away
To
Safe holes.

Chase
After
Them,
So fast!

You can have more than one word in any line, like **S**afe holes and **S**o fast! But the first word in each line must start with the letter from the up-and-down word. You might try using your name. Make each line say something essential about yourself and your feelings.

Dear T,

Here's another word game that's fun. You can get lots of ideas for poems from this one.

A Game: *Word Box*

It's a game with lots of words, called *Word Box*. It is also sometimes called *Word Bowl*.

<u>Using This Book.</u> On each of pages 12 through 15 are three columns of words. Take this book to a copy machine and make copies of those pages. Then cut the copy of each page into columns and each column into rows, so that you have lots of slips of paper with words on them. Pinch each one in the middle of the back, so that it's not too easy to see the words. The slips should all look as though they come from Chinese fortune cookies. Put all of the slips in a cardboard box, like a shoe box, or in a bowl. A shoe box is good because it has a top; so you won't lose slips when you're not using them.

Each person playing the game takes a dozen slips of paper.
After that the rules of the game are really simple: ANYTHING GOES! Try to arrange the slips into a poem. Make plural any word that you want to. Change around any verb, adding "es" or "ing." If a word, like "travel" can be used as either a noun or a verb, use it whichever way you want.

If the word on one of the slips doesn't work, trade it for another, or just leave it out. If more than one person is playing, offer a slip that you don't want to the others. Add any words that you want. The slips are only intended to give you the idea for a poem. They are not supposed to limit you at all. You just might be able to find a poem in the slips, because they all came from poems written by young people about your age.

Using a Computer. If you know how to use a spreadsheet program on a computer, you don't have to do all the copying and cutting. Type all of the words in a column. In the cell next to the top word type "@rand" (if you use LOTUS 1-2-3, or the equivalent if you use EXCEL.) Next, copy "@rand" all the way down to the cell next to the bottom word. Now sort the two columns together, using the "@rand" column as the primary-key. You'll get a different twelve words at the top of the column every time you sort. Write them down, and see what you can do with them.

FLATTEN	FALL	UNDER
GENTLY	DEAD	BLUE
MOANING	BRUSH	SENT
NATURE	SISTER	SUMMERTIME
SOMETIME	FEEL LIKE	PLAY
SALTY	STARE	SING
HEAR	CRYING	RULED
RELATIVE	PALE	SHY
WISH	ROCK	NEW
DRIP	FOOD	EYE
NECK	DANCE	MELT
SUN	BACK	PAPER
SIT	COUNTRY	COME
STOMACH	HAWK	PURPLE
ELSE	LETTER	CRASH
BOY	LIKE A FLOWER	HEART
SAIL	CUP	EXPRESSION
TEMPLE	CLIFF	ROOT
CARTON	HARD	THOUGHT
BREAD	ABOUT	BLACK
BRAIN	EAT	ANT
WATERY	RECORDING	MOVING
SPIDER	BEFORE	MISTY
HAPPINESS	REALIZE	I AM
CONNECTED	MOUNTAIN	MAD
PINK	GOOD	BAG
CHIN	FACE	CANNOT
HAPPEN	FEEL	BEAT
PEOPLE	SHOW	YOU AND I
GOLDFISH	DOVE	JUICE
DRESSING	CRYSTAL	PET
SWOOPS	ENDLESS	FAR
DOWN	STREAM	RUN
BATH	BOWL	WINTER
IDEA	RAIN	BEYOND
LICK	THROUGH	RUSH

KITTEN'S PAWS	DRESS	HOPE
HILL	PANIC	SWEET
LISTEN	FIVE	HOW
THEM	WATER	WAKE
HAIR	OUT OF	LITTLE
PIG	WHENEVER	SUMMER
WRITE	KING	TURN
SMARTNESS	LONELY	LAUGH
TIP	HAND	GET
UNCLE	LILY PAD	CHERRY
PIECE	YOU/I SEE	DESPAIR
BONE	LIKE A STREAM	ONE
RAINBOWS	WET	FROG
PUDDING	SEA	GREY
ANCIENT	TAPE	BORN
THEN	RECORDER	NO ONE
STICK	CLAM	TRAILING
COLD	SLIDE	DIFFERENT
TUNNEL	AROUND	LIKE FRIENDS
EVERYTHING	REAL LIFE	LACE UP
PORCH	OPENED	BECAUSE
TUMBLE	NEW MOTHER	NOISE
TIRE	FLOWER	BREAK
SHINE	STORM CLOUD	FOREST
ONLY	TOWN	SHIP
QUESTIONS	GLASS	WHEN
LOVE	DRUM	ARRIVE
DIE	MANY	FILL WITH
EARTH	TIME	SIGH
CLAW	LEAF	BALL
ACROSS	WORD	WHITE
WHY	ANGRY	JOIN
PUMPING	LOVE	BROWN
CREEP UP	WEB	MORNING
BEHIND	RED	CHILDREN
CHEEK	BRING	EAGLE

AS IF	SAD	ANYTHING
NEST	AS LONG AS	MOON
AWAY	MOOD	GOES
DREAM	GROUND	BLOOD
PLAIN	LOST	SOMETHING
SILVER	SPROUT	STOVE
VOICE	CENTER	YOUR HEART
SEND	STRONG	SHADOW
SCARE	DAY	COBWEB
BURN	SOUND	SOFT
HE	STEM	SINK
TEACH	CAT	THINK
SPOT	SALAMI	SLIPPERY
LIKE LOVE	LIKE PLANES	LEAVE
WIGGLE	ROUND	LIFT
WOLVES	MAGIC	TEA KETTLE
LIKE FLOWERS	MYSTERIOUS	THING
LIKE A WORM	CHIP	HANG
UNDERSTAND	SEE	BUSY
FIRE	DRY	SPRING
TUBE	BELONG	MY PENCIL
HOUSE	LIKE THE SUN	NIGHT
WOOD	CANNON	CLOSE
CAGE	BARREL	STAR LIGHT
BITE	MOUTH	TEETH
HEAD	HAPPY	AGAIN
GUITAR	DRUNK	FLY
FROM	AIRPORT	TINY
ROAD	TOOTHPASTE	SADNESS
LIKE A BUD	WORLD	POT
OUTSIDE	WATER-BUG	SNOW BALL
JAR	SPEAK	LIKE A WALK
GIRL	EMERALD	CATCH
STORM	JUST	END
SANDWICH	MACHINE	GRASS
WHALE	BLOW	WIND

NEVER	AGAINST	SEED
NIGHTMARE	ANSWER	GROW
CHEEP	REACH	SNOW
STOP	CLOUD	THREAD
DINOSAUR	WIDE	ALL
CRUMPLE	DRINK	FAR AWAY
BASEBALL	RABBIT	WING
MOLD	FUR	SHAPE
LIKE SUNSHINE	NOBODY	SAND
TOMORROW	WASH	BOTTLE
BUMP	LIKE FINGERS	SET
WILD	ANYBODY	WHOLE WORLD
DARK	SUNFLOWER	CAR
CRACK	HIT	TOE
STRING	MOVIE	TALK
PINE CONE	GIGGLE	IN SEARCH OF
APPLE	TRUST	BUNNY
TOUCH	DIAMOND	LONG
LEG	UNIVERSE	HEAVILY
DOWN	TWO	THAT
RAGE	LIKE SNOW	LAND
EGG	WONDER	BODY
ANIMAL	SEA SHELL	LIKE RAIN
IN ORDER	YELLOW	PIERCE
BIG	TRY TO	LENGTHY
LOOK AT	OCEAN	RELEASE
CUCKOO	LOOK LIKE	HOLLOW
SPECIAL	SCALE	MOTH
ELSEWHERE	TAKE	FINGERNAIL
SILLY	FLUTTER	SHARP
GRAND	FLESH	FRESH
CREAK	SNAKE	REST OF
YOU/I WANT	SMELL	HARD ROCKS
TOGETHER	KIND	NEXT
EMBARRASS	LIGHT	LOOK AT
LIKE AN APPLE	POETRY	ROOM

A random sorting of words from the *Word Box* produced these:

BOTTLE
SCALE
STAR LIGHT
SAND
SIT
KITTEN'S PAWS
TOWN
CENTER
TEACH
EAGLE
CLOUD
LACE UP

What pictures do these words make you see? A bottle of sand someone took home from the beach? Is the bottle sitting on a weighing scale? Or are the bottle and a fish scale lying on the sand?

Do you see star light shining on the center of a town? Of course you see a kitten's paws, and maybe an eagle flying among clouds. Do you see shoelaces, in their typical back and forth pattern? A cardboard with holes and laces running through them to make a design? A teacher sitting in class? Is there any common thread running through them?

Is star light an idea that could bind these sights together? Maybe something like this (notice that the word bottle is left out and other words are added):

Star Light

Star light
Sits softly
As kittens' paws
On the center
Of the town,
Shines the sand
Bright as
Fish scales, and
Teaches eagles
Where to lace up
Clouds.

Dear T,

About a *Journal*

There are many other places that you can get *ideas* for poems. You might start a *journal* for yourself. It doesn't have to be a talky diary. You can just keep in it notes about things that happen that matter to you. Then from time to time you can make lists of your good times and bad times and the changes in your life. Your good and bad times, the changes in your life, and the lessons you learn from them are often the starting points for poem ideas.

More About *Ideas* for Poems

A lot of poems are written about what you see or hear or even smell, often in nature. Such things are great if they seem to have a special meaning, or if they can be compared to something else.

Many poems tell stories, like the nursery rhymes. You can get *ideas* for poems from other poems and from songs.

About an *Idea File*

Keep an *idea file*. Note in your *idea file* anything that seems strange or significant, any comparison that seems unique. Make lists of sights and sounds and smells, perhaps from nature. Across from them on the page write down things that seem like them.

Note anything that is like a riddle or gives you joy or makes you angry. Write down ideas for poems whenever they pop into your head. Write down rhymes that you like, or even just word patterns that sound nice to you.

If you get an idea in the middle of the night, get up and make a note of it in your *idea file*. It's easier to do that than it is to get up and write the poem, itself. And you really don't want to forget it!

Try out your *idea file* on pages provided in the back of the book.

Dear T,

The dome-in-Rome poem was fun! From talking to you, it's clear that you have all kinds of poem ideas in your head. You've asked what your poems might look like and whether they could be short or would have to be long?

A Short Poem

> The poems that you write can be short
> If you're of an impatient sort.

There! You see! You don't have to be long and wordy. (That's so short that it doesn't even count.) Seriously, let me tell you about a special kind of short poem.

About **Haiku** and **Senryu** and *Syllables*

These next poems are really short. They're almost all about things that you see. They are a Japanese poem form called **haiku** or **senryu**. They always have seventeen *syllables*.

You know what *syllables* are. They are the parts into which you can break a spoken word. You can tell what the *syllables* of a word are by saying it. Take, for example, the word *syllables*, itself. Sound it out:

> *syl* • *la* • *bles*

If you clap your hands while saying the word, you'll want to clap three times, once with each *syllable*.

Syllables can be just one letter, like the middle "i" in "indefinite".

in • def • i • nite

Or they can be the whole word, like the words "this" and "that".

Haiku and **senryu** poems have five *syllables* in the first line, seven in the second, and five in the third -- seventeen in all. It doesn't matter where the emphasis is. They do not have any rhymes.

The only difference between **haiku** and **senryu** is that **senryu** are funny. **Haiku** and **senryu** poems express a connection you see or a feeling you have about something.

Here are **haiku** about some of the things that we saw here in Puget Sound in the last year.

Puget Sound Scenes

Sunlight shining through
Iced branches and spider webs:
Winter morning lace.

In the thick grey fog
A boy can be an island,
Until it burns off.

The South wind, blowing
Spindrift, wraps the black waters
With bright, white ribbons.

Through glistening waters,
Framed in fall reds and yellows,
Tridents come and go.

In summer sun Blue
Angels climb and climb, then swing
Down the curve of sky.

Try this:

Go through one of the **haiku** poems above. Divide each line into *syllables* with a vertical line, like this:

>   Sun ¦ light ¦ shin ¦ ing ¦ through
>   Iced ¦ branch ¦ es ¦ and ¦ spi ¦ der ¦ webs:
>   Win ¦ ter ¦ morn ¦ ing ¦ lace.

Count up the *syllables* on each line, and see if the number is right.

✉ ✉ ✉

Dear T,

You've asked how poems compared things with one another. The first three haiku in **Puget Sound Scenes** each compared the image that it described to something else.

> The iced branches and spider webs look like lace.

> A boy, alone in the fog, is like an island.

> The white foam, blown down the backs of waves, looks like white, giftwrap ribbons.

The next senryu poem also make a comparison.

> The cars' movements in a parking lot are like a dance.

A Senryu

"After you, Madam."
"No! I want your parking space."
Parking lot polka.

About *Similes* and *Metaphors*

You know what the word "similar" means. It means that something is like something else. For example, on a rainy day, a tree can be similar to an umbrella. In poetry when you say that something is like something else, it is called a *simile*, almost the same word. A poet a long time ago wrote one of the most famous of all *similes*, "My love is like a red, red rose." If he had left out the word "like," "My love is a red, red rose," it would have been called a *metaphor*. *Metaphors* are just *similes* without the words "like" or "as."

Similes and *metaphors* compare things with one another. Many, many poems contains *similes* and *metaphors*, like the haiku and senryu that you have just read. The best *similes* and *metaphors* make the reader stop and say to himself, "That's right. I never thought of that."

Haiku Metaphor

> A kernel of truth
> Linking man, time and nature:
> Haiku metaphor.

In deciding what comparison to use, try to think through all aspects of the comparison. Suppose you wanted to compare love to a body of water in the first line of a haiku. Which of the following should you use?

> Love is the ocean
> Our love is the sea
> Love is a river

Oceans have tides that rise and fall. Do you want to say that love is greater at some times than at others? Seas and oceans can both be calm or stormy. Love can be that way, too. Oceans surround the land. Seas are more contained, either by the land or partially by the land and partially by the ocean. Rivers run through the land. Any one of those ideas could be right, depending upon what you want to say.

Try this:

Since we've already talked about love, let's talk about anger. Which of the following comparisons do you think are right?

<u>If "yes," why?</u>

Anger is a thunder storm _____

      a tornado _____

      an ice storm _____

Anger is a shark _____

      a lion _____

      a vulture _____

Anger is a _____ _____

      a _____ _____

      a _____ _____

About *Capital Letters*

You may have noticed that the first letter in each line is a *capital*. That's the way poems are most often written, but it is not a rule. A famous modern poet named e. e. cummings never used *capitals* at all. Not even in his own name. Try not using *capitals* in your **haiku** or **senryu** poems. Because the Japanese written language is made up of characters rather than letters, they don't use *capitals*. You might find that not using *capitals* will add something to your poem. For example, if we take the *capitals* out of the **haiku** about the Blue Angels flying team, it becomes:

in summer sun blue
angels climb and climb, then swing
down the curve of sky.

Now we have to ask whether the blue angels might be Heavenly angels. Are they wearing blue gowns? Blue jeans? Are they sad? How could they be sad if they are having so much fun?

28

Dear T,

It's great that you're interested in **haiku**. Thank you so much for the two that you've given me. They are both very nice nature poems. It was really interesting watching the mantas feeding at the sea wall, wasn't it? They're so graceful. You said that you read in a magazine article about a manta that has a wingspread of twenty feet. That's wide enough, tip to tip, to go across two lanes of highway. Enormous! It must weigh tons. Thanks for passing on the information.

Sunsets

by T

Sunsets are so cool,
They rule! The best of all is
The lipstick sunset.

Manta Rays

by T

Manta rays glide fast,
Swooping, flying, diving through
Hawaii waters.

Dear T,

Certainly we can try to create a **haiku** or **senryu** poem together. Your idea that we might be able to make a poem out of a riddle is a good one. Maybe they can provide good ideas, particularly for **senryu**, because they're funnier. Do you remember the riddle, "What has four or more wheels and flies?" It was popular long ago. In those days airplanes had only three wheels. Maybe we can turn it into a **senryu**.

Wheels and Flies

What ¦ has ¦ four ¦ or ¦ more	5
Wheels ¦ and ¦ flies?	3
A ¦ gar¦bage ¦ truck.	4

The first line is five *syllables*; so it's all right. But the second line is only three *syllables*; so it is four short. And the third is four *syllables*, one short. We can lengthen the second line by moving up the words from the last line. We can create a new last line that brings the riddle into the modern world.

Wheels and Flies

What has four or more	5
Wheels and flies? A garbage truck?	7
Seven-four-seven!	5

Here are some other classic riddles.

"What flies forever and rests never?"
　　Answer: the wind.

"What has one voice and yet becomes four-footed, then two-footed, and then three-footed?"
　　Answer: man, who crawls as a baby, then walks upright, and then walks with a cane.

"When is a door not a door?"
　　Answer: "When it is ajar."

"What has eyes but cannot see?"
　　Answer: a potato.

"What kind of fruit is red when it is green?"
　　Answer: a blackberry.

I know you can make a **haiku** or **senryu** out of one or two of them or out of a comparison, a *simile* or *metaphor*, of your own.

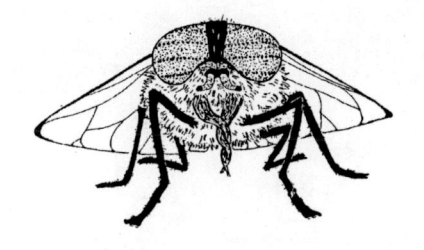

Dear T,

Do you remember my comment that you could get the idea for a poem from a song. Listen to songs. Most of them are poems set to music. Here's a poem that was suggested by an old song that started, "Yes, we have no bananas. We have no bananas today."

Sharing

Yes, we have a banana,
Said T to C, said he.
Yes, we have a banana,
We have a banana or three.
There is one here for you,
And another for me,
And the third we will share, as you'll see.

With respect to the third,
I will say a brief word.
In a trice I will slice
It; you'll see just how nice
It will be.

Here's a thick slice for you,
And two thin ones for me,
And two more just for you,
And another for me.
So this plate is your share,
And well pleased you should be.
It was all very fair,
As I'm sure you'll agree.

Some will share by the weight;
Some according to need;
Some will share by the measure;
Some without care or heed.
Just how it is done does not really matter,
If I'm the divider, and your share is fatter.

Dear T,

You've asked about the words that are in some of the poems. Some of them are pretty old fashioned, like "trice". They're in there, really, just because they rhyme or fit the form. Really the best words to use are the ones that you hear every day.

Getting the Word

Listen to the way people talk.
Listen to the words that they use,
As during the day you walk
About or watch the TeVening news.

Above all, dear T, read!
Read with greed.
Become a collector of words,
'Til, like a cage full of birds,
They chirp for attention
And at least a mention.

Then let the rhymes play
   Around in your head;
     Think of each phrase,
All during the day,
   And as you lie in bed,
     'Til it drives you craz-
yyyyyyyyyyyyyyyyyyyyyyyyy.

You'll want to expel them,
Write 'em down, throw 'em out,
Even if you misspell them,
Of that I've no doubt.

Dear T,

Here's a short one. The idea for this one came from another book of poems for kids by Shel Silverstein.

Do You Drink Up or Down?

T drinks his sodas up;
He drinks his med'cine down.
Sometimes he likes to do it
The other way around.
It matters very little;
It all goes to his middle.

Next is another short poem for you. It shows how sometimes you can twist around an old saying and turn it into a funny poem.

Flies Time

The very next time
    You're having a ball,
Take a look and you'll see
    By the clock on the wall
A couple of flies
    Just watching it run,
Which shows you flies time,
    When you're having fun.

There are lots of old sayings that you can twist around for a laugh. Ben Franklin said, "time is money." You could switch the words around in a poem in which a thief learns that stealing money means time in prison.

Another trick you can use is switching the sounds of the words' first letters. For example, suppose that when Ben Franklin was in Europe as America's Ambassador during the Revolutionary War, he met a street actor. The actor's face was covered with white makeup. He didn't say anything. He just made exaggerated movements and gestures. Eventually Ben Franklin said, impatiently, "Time is money." In response the actor, speaking for the first time, introduced himself: "Mime is Tony."

Here are some other sayings that you can have fun with:

> "A fool and his money are soon parted."

> "Necessity is the mother of invention."

> "People who live in glass houses should not throw stones."

> "A word to the wise is sufficient."

To make one of these into a poem, decide what words or sounds you want to switch. Then set the scene, tell the story, and spring the trap in the last line or two.

Dear T,

The next is a poem about one of my problems. Do you remember the nursery rhyme about the old man who was snoring? The end of this poem also twists around an old expression, and that helps it to be funny.

Snoring

When it's time for my rest,
I'm afraid that I'll snore
And my snorts and my snuffles
Make me sound like a boar.
My good wife has told me,
"It's your snore I abhor,
That loud noise in the night
That I cannot ignore.
"If you will just fix it,
Though it will be a chore,
I know that I'll love you,
Adore you, evermore."
A request such as that
I just cannot ignore.

Now, I lie on my side
So as not to snore more.
So as not to be near
I could lie on the floor
Or in bed somewhere else
That's behind a closed door.
Of devices to cure it
I have tried a galore:
Things to open my nose
More than it was before.
Do not breathe through my nose?
But that's what it is for!

It's the slack in the palate
That's the cause of the roar.
A good doc with a laser
Could cut it to the core,
But my throat would be, Oh!
So exceedingly sore.

So I looked for a doc
Who would know what to do.
I was lucky to find
One, by name: Doctor Pew.
He would straighten my septum.
The result would be splendid.
So he broke and reset it;
Then he sewed it and splinted.

The hard splint in my nose
Was a real irritation.
In a week it became
A profound aggravation.
So I went to the doctor
And said, "Don't you suppose
That I'd like you to get
Your business out of my nose?"

Dear T:

Here's something you might enjoy. Take a look at a book of puns. A great book of puns and pun games is *Get Thee to a Punnery* by Richard Lederer (Wyrick & Co., 1988). Puns are words with similar spelling or sounds but different meanings. For example, a motel was called the "Dew Drop Inn." Compare that with "Do Drop In." The first is cute, and it suggests the second. A famous tire company ad showed a child in a night shirt with a candle. The slogan beneath it was "Time to re-tire." The play is between "retire," meaning to go to sleep, and "re-tire," meaning to buy a new tire. Mr. Lederer notes in one of his games the several meanings the word "ring" has, which led to this.

Rings

A ring can fit on a finger;
A ring can sound in the ear;
Two boxers will fight in a ring
That is not round but square;
And rings surround some planets
Quite far away from here.

"So ring me up," she said,
"Your voice I'd love to hear."
"Give me a ring," she said,
"To wear in my long, dark hair."
"Thanks for the ring," she said,
"That plights our troth, My Dear."

As you've already noticed, there's a pun in the title of this book. There is a pun in **The Empty Store**, which comes next. There is also one in **The Mechanical-Minded Trojan**: Troy-sickle and tricycle, which you'll come to later. You'll probably find others. Anyway, see if the Lederer book or another on puns gives you some that can be shaped into poems, like **Rings**.

The pun on which this next poem is based is between the word "empty" and the made-up word "emptee."

42

The Empty Store

Now if a seller's called "vendor"
And if a buyer's called "vendee,"
That buyer buys what seller "vends"
Is all quite clear and plain to see.

But, T, you know you must take care
Lest goods you've bought aren't good but poor.
The warning's in the Latin phrase
That means "beware," "Caveat emptor."

Now if a buyer's called "emptor,"
Then surely seller is "emptee."
But if he is "emptee," he'll close
And take a plane to Waikiki.

Dear T,

Our afternoon together last Saturday was really nice. It was fun walking along the Gig Harbor waterfront, tossing rhymes back and forth.

About *Rhymes*

Let's talk about *rhymes*. You already have a good idea what they are. Basically, they are words that end with the same sound. But you might ask, "Thinking up *rhymes* is hard. Why bother?" It's a good question, because most poems written by young people these days have no *rhymes*. There are two answers.

First, it can help you get an idea for a poem. When someone asked the famous poet William Butler Yeats where his ideas came from, he answered, "The *rhymes*." You'll see how ideas can come from *rhymes* when we get to **The Boy from Calcutta**. Second, it adds to the fun of a poem. Most songs are poems with rhymes. They're written that way because the audience likes them better. And *rhyming* adds to your pride in your poem when you've finished it. If the nursery *rhymes* didn't *rhyme*, would you remember them?

The next poem has lots and lots of *rhymes* in it. There are single syllables *rhymes*, like care and despair. It doesn't matter that "despair" is a two syllable word, as long as the emphasis is on the last syllable, and it sounds the same as "care."

Notice that these two *rhyming* words, care and despair, do not have the same spelling. It's the sound that matters, not the spelling. Sometimes you can have fun changing spelling, as was done with **TeVening** news and **wareplane**.

About *Double Syllable Rhymes*

There are also *double syllable rhymes*, like Pacific and specific. Here both the sound and the spelling are the same. The effect of *double syllable rhymes* is to startle the reader, and often to get a laugh. When you have a *double syllable rhyme*, both words do not have to be two syllable words. One or both of the *double syllable rhymes* can be made up of two words.

About *True Rhymes* and *Near Rhymes*

This brings up another aspect of *rhymes*. The *rhymes* that we have been talking about are "true" *rhymes*. They really sound like each other, like care and despair. *True rhymes* relate lines to one another, almost like punctuation marks.

On the other hand, for someone with a sharp ear splendid and splinted in **Snoring** only sort of sound like each other. Compare the words "did" and "said." Words that only sort of sound like one another are called *near rhymes* or *slant rhymes*. *Near rhymes* allow you to slip past them and go on to the next line. They may startle a reader who's expecting a *true rhyme*.

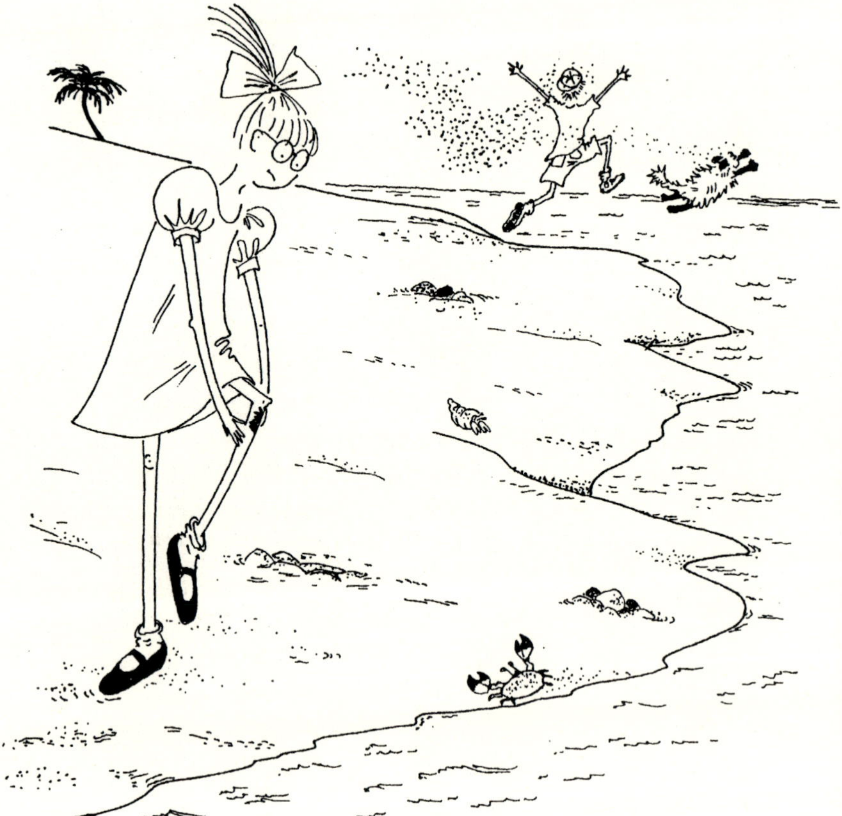

Please!

On an island in the Pacific,
On Pitcairn to be specific,
The inhabitants never swear.
Instead they say, *"Please!"*
Whether for anger or care,
They only say, *"Please!"*
Whether for fear or despair,
They only say, *"Please!"*
Instead of the "F" word or "D" word,
They only say, *"Please!"*
Instead of the "S" word or "B" word,
They only say, *"Please!"*

They say, *"Please!"* with inflection,
With force and direction.
Examples are these:
If hikers are lost in the trees,
They merely call, **"Please!"**
If a boy's stung by bees,
He simply cries, **"Please!"**
If a girl skins her knees,
She only moans, *"Please!"*
If in an argument one disagrees,
The other shouts, **"Please!"**

You don't have to swear
To be understood.
There are other words
That will do just as [~~good~~] well.
(Oh, *please*! It doesn't rhyme.
I'll have to do better next time.)

How many other words can you think of that *rhyme* with **please**? There are lots.

> Did you think of these words that rhyme with **please**: breeze, cheese, fleas, freeze, wheeze, keys, Japanese, Siamese, peas, trapeze, squeeze, sneeze, seize, and tweeze (you know, what tweezers do)?

You can find many more in rhyming dictionaries. See if you can make up another stanza or two that describe times when Pitcairners might say "please."

About *Stanzas*

A *stanza*, by the way, is just a group of lines in a poem set apart from other lines by space, usually a blank line. The above poem has three *stanzas*. *Stanzas* act like paragraphs on a page or chapters in a book. They break up the poem into digestible bits.

Look at the poem **Snoring**, which you've already read. The first *stanza* is 12 lines. The second is 20 lines. The rest of the poem is two *stanzas* of eight lines each. Which part was easier to read?

Also, you can use *stanzas* to shift scene, focus, mood or time. In **Snoring** the first *stanza* describes the problem. The second *stanza* describes possible solutions, and the third *stanza* describes the solution chosen. And the fourth *stanza* describes the new problem and leads up to and gives the punch line.

Did you think of lines like:

They grumble "`Please`"	They call out "`Please`"
When scratching for fleas.	In the midst of a sneeze.
Old ones say "`Please`"	They holler out "`Please,`"
With a snort or a wheeze.	If there's too much breeze.

Dear T,

A Game: *Football*

Here's a game you can play to have fun with rhymes. Did you ever hear comedians Hudson and Landry's bit called the "Soul Bowl?" In it sportscaster Ace Grovnik interviews foot ball coach Blueberry Hill. Blueberry names the players on his roster. They include:

> Lima Bean Green,   All the Way Grey,
> Split the Scene Dean,   The Real Don Steel,
> Tyrone Thone, and   Save Us Davis,

You can make a photocopy of the football team roster form on the next two pages. Take a phone book and get the last names of your players from it. Write them in the LAST NAME column. If you're playing with someone else, switch sheets. Next, pick a name for your team. Then give the players nicknames that rhyme with their last names. For extra credit you can also give the offensive and defensive lines rhyming nicknames. Here's the scoring:

If a nickname is a:	You score a:		
Double Syllable True Rhyme	Touchdown	6	points
Single Syllable True Rhyme	Field Goal	3	points
Double Syllable Near Rhyme	Field Goal	3	points
Single Syllable Near Rhyme	Extra Point	1	points
Names with Alliteration	Extra Point	1	point
A Rhyme that doesn't	Safety	-2	points

Other rules: Double syllable rhymes can be two syllables that both rhyme with the last syllable of the last name, like "Down Town Brown" (true rhymes, so a touchdown) or two syllables that rhyme with two syllables of the last name, like "Save Us Davis" (near rhymes, so only a field goal.) Remember, you can't have extra points without touchdowns; so there can be no more extra points than there are touchdowns.

FOOTBALL

TEAM:	NICKNAME	LAST NAME	Points
POSITION			
COACH			
OFFENSIVE LINE			
WIDE RECEIVER			
LEFT TACKLE			
LEFT GUARD			
CENTER			
RIGHT GUARD			
RIGHT TACKLE			
TIGHT END			
WIDE RECEIVER			
QUARTER BACK			
RUNNING BACK			
FULL BACK			

DEFENSIVE LINE														
LEFT END														
LEFT TACKLE														
RIGHT TACKLE														
RIGHT END														
LINEBACKER														
LINEBACKER														
LINEBACKER														
LEFT CORNER														
RIGHT CORNER														
SAFETY														
SAFETY														
KICKER														
												TOTAL POINTS:		

Dear T,

About *Alliteration*

When we were talking about rhymes, we were talking about the sounds at the ends of words. How about the sounds at the beginning of words? You can have fun with those, too. When words have the same sound at the beginning, it's called ***alliteration***. The most famous example is:

> The Austrian army, awfully arrayed,
> Boldly besieged embattled Belgrade.

Most of the words in the first line start with an *a* sound. Most of the words in the second line start with a *b*. In the next poem there are words starting with *c, d, p, r, f, b, n, f, w, w* and *h* that work together. (A **codger** is an older person. A person's **dotage** is his or her very senior years.)

The Recluse

A codger called Cooper constructed a cottage.
He decided to dwell there during his dotage.
He properly plastered and painted it puce.
He'd reside there alone and remain a recluse.
He filled it with furniture he got from his father,
And a bed that he bought from his baby brother.

Then he met a nice nurse whose nickname was Nella.
If she fell for him, he'd be one fortunate fella.
He wooed her and won her, though some wondered why
She would want to be wed to such a weird guy.
But how happy he was, just holding her hand,
Which shows how a woman can change a man's plan.

Try this:

Put together groups of words, each starting with the same sound, that might be things in your room or things in your yard.

Sound: _____   **Sound:** _____

Words: _____   *Words:* _____

_____   _____

_____   _____

_____   _____

See the fun you can have with it. There are lots more.

Alliteration adds humor, melody and strength to a line. Compare the following lines with the lines at the top of the page:

Compare: The Viennese soldiers, terribly arrayed,
Daringly attacked old war torn Belgrade.

With: The Austrian army, awfully arrayed,
Boldly besieged embattled Belgrade.

Compare: An old man named Wilson built himself a cottage.
He wanted to live there during his old age.

With: A codger called Cooper constructed a cottage.
He decided to dwell there during his dotage.

Without the *alliteration*, the lines seem dull and weak.

More About *Football*

Here's another way that you can get extra points playing *Football*. Blueberry Hill named some of the other players on his team, including

Homesick Harris

A nickname that starts with the same sound as the last name is good for an extra point, in addition to any other points it may earn for rhymes.

Dear T,

Thank you very much for your poem about whales.

Whales!

by T

Whales have such wonderful tails.
They splash, and they jump, and they play.
They swim all about so that people won't doubt
That whales can play every day.

We've already talked about *rhymes*. You've got a good *rhyme* at the end of the second and fourth lines.

> play and day

You've also got some nice *internal rhymes* in **Whales!**

> Whales and tails
> about and doubt
> play and day

Your poem is a lot of fun. When a family of Orca whales is cavorting, it certainly looks like play. Your repetition of the word play emphasizes this.

About *Repetition*

Repetition is one of a poet's absolutely most powerful tools. It not only adds emphasis, it hammers it. Supposing that you were going to write a three stanza poem about getting lost on a snowy night, then seeing a familiar sight, and finally the comfort of being home again. If you started each stanza with It was snowing... or ended it with And it snowed, you'd have even the readers thinking their own feet were cold. For another example, look at the poem **Please!** on page 47.

Dear T,

Here's a limerick. Again, the point is playing with words.

A Salesman's Advice

A good salesman was heard to explain
Why he never shipped wares on a train:
"To show buyers I care
I will send goods by air,
From warehouse to their house by wareplane!"

If a salesman keeps his wares in a warehouse, why wouldn't he ship them on a wareplane? There's no limit to the games that you can play with words, and a poem is a great place to do it. I hope that you liked this one.

Dear T,

The other night at the zoo you suggested that we make up a poem about an elephant, but call it an "ephelant." You have great ideas! Here's a limerick about an "ephelant." This one emphasizes alliteration.

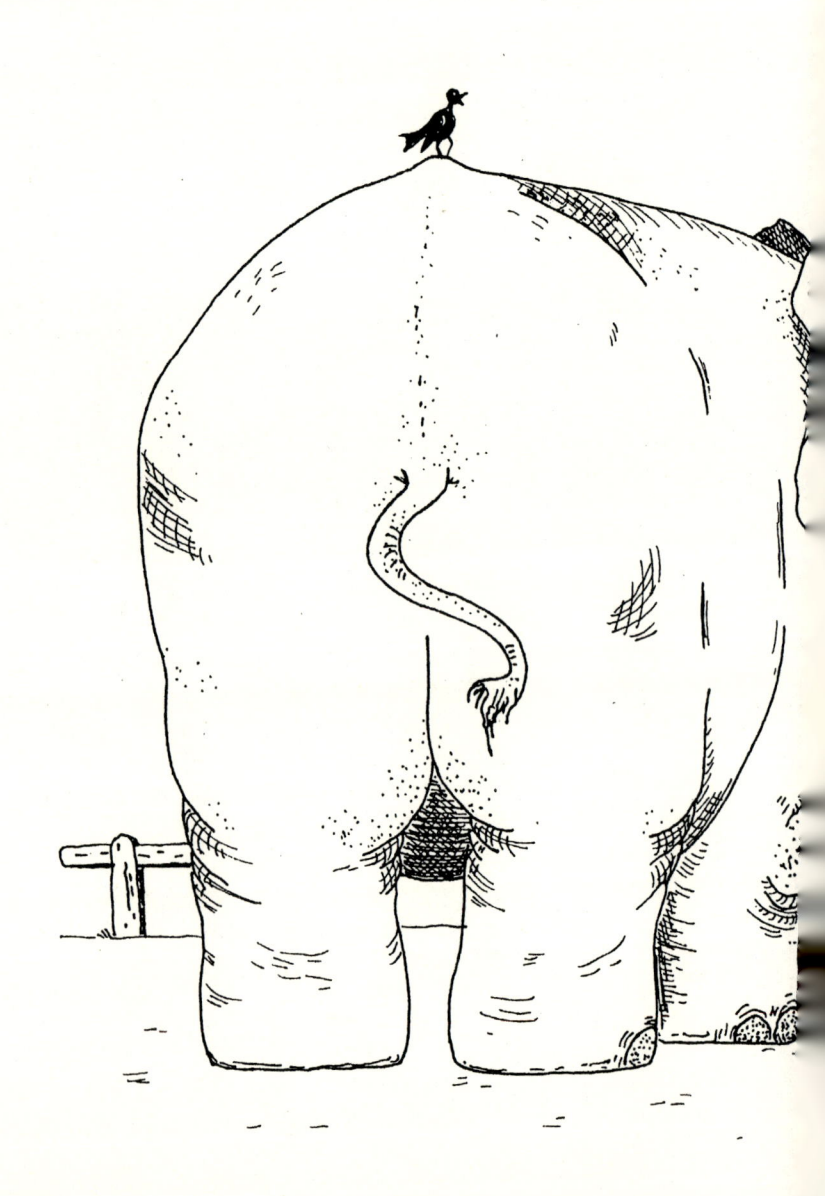

Ephphie, the Ephelant

Here's a story of "Ephphie, the Ephelant."
Almost epherywhere that old Ephphie went
She would use her long nose
Just the same as a hose
And spray epheryone with the ephluent.

About Limericks

Since we've had a couple of **limericks**, let's talk about **limericks**. **Limericks** can be about anything that you can imagine, as long as it's fun. **Limericks** with word tricks in them, like **wareplane** and **ephelant**, are good fun.

What makes a **limerick** a **limerick**? Two things. First the rhyme pattern. As you'll see, the words at the end of the first, second and fifth lines rhyme: **Ephelant, Ephphie went,** and **ephluent**. (In this case one's a near rhyme.) The third and fourth lines also rhyme: **nose** and **hose**. This is called an *a,a,b,b,a* pattern. The sound at the end of each line is given a letter. If it rhymes with an earlier line, it's given the same letter as the earlier line. Here's another example: **d'Orso, torso** and **more-so** all rhyme. So do **that** and **fat**.

About *Meter*

The second thing that makes a **limerick** a **limerick** is the rhythm. In poetry the rhythm is called *meter*. The *meter* refers to the pattern of syllables and the emphasis given to certain syllables. We talked about syllables before. The syllables are divided up into groups that are called feet. Every foot has at least one syllable that is emphasized.

The rhythm or *meter* of a **limerick** makes is possible to clap in time or even to sing it. Try clapping to these lines. Clap on the syllables that are printed in **bold** type.

The Mechanical-Minded Trojan

Did a **Tro**jan with **mind** quite me**chan**ical
Fabri**cate** the first **har**vester **ve**hicle
With three **wheels** and a **seat**
And a **blade** to cut **neat**,
Which they **cer**tainly **called** a Troy-**sick**le?

An Opera Diva Named d'Orso

An **op**era **d**iva named **d'Or**so
Pos**sessed** a most **trou**blesome **tor**so.
Though she **tried** this and **that**
To get **rid** of her **fat**,
Her **tor**so got **more**-so and **more**-so.

As you can see from the number of bold syllables in the last two poems, the first two lines and the last line each have three feet. The third and fourth line each have two feet.

In **limericks** each of the feet has three syllables. In **The Mechanical-Minded Trojan** the first two syllables of each foot are not emphasized. The third syllable is emphasized. Do you hear the drumbeat on **Tro** and **mind** and **chan**? The name for this kind of a foot is an *Anapest*.

It doesn't matter that there are a syllable or two hanging over at the end of the line as long as they are not emphasized. It also doesn't matter if a foot ends in the middle of a word. The next foot can begin right there. There's an example:

and some **nog**¦gins of **grog**.

in the second line of the next **limerick**. In this next **limerick** the vertical lines | show how the feet divide up.

The Witch's Brew

The old **witch** ¦ in her **brew** ¦ dropped a **frog**,
Two or **three**, ¦ and some **nog**¦gins of **grog**.
   Said **she**, "When ¦ I **blend** it,
   It's **going** to ¦ be **splen**did.
The **coven**'ll ¦ be **lovin**' ¦ my **frog** grog nog."

In the last three lines of this **limerick** each of the feet has the emphasis on the middle syllable, just like the first two lines and the last line of **An Opera Diva Named d'Orso**. Can you feel the drumbeat on **she, blend, going** and **splen**? This foot is called an *Amphibrach*.

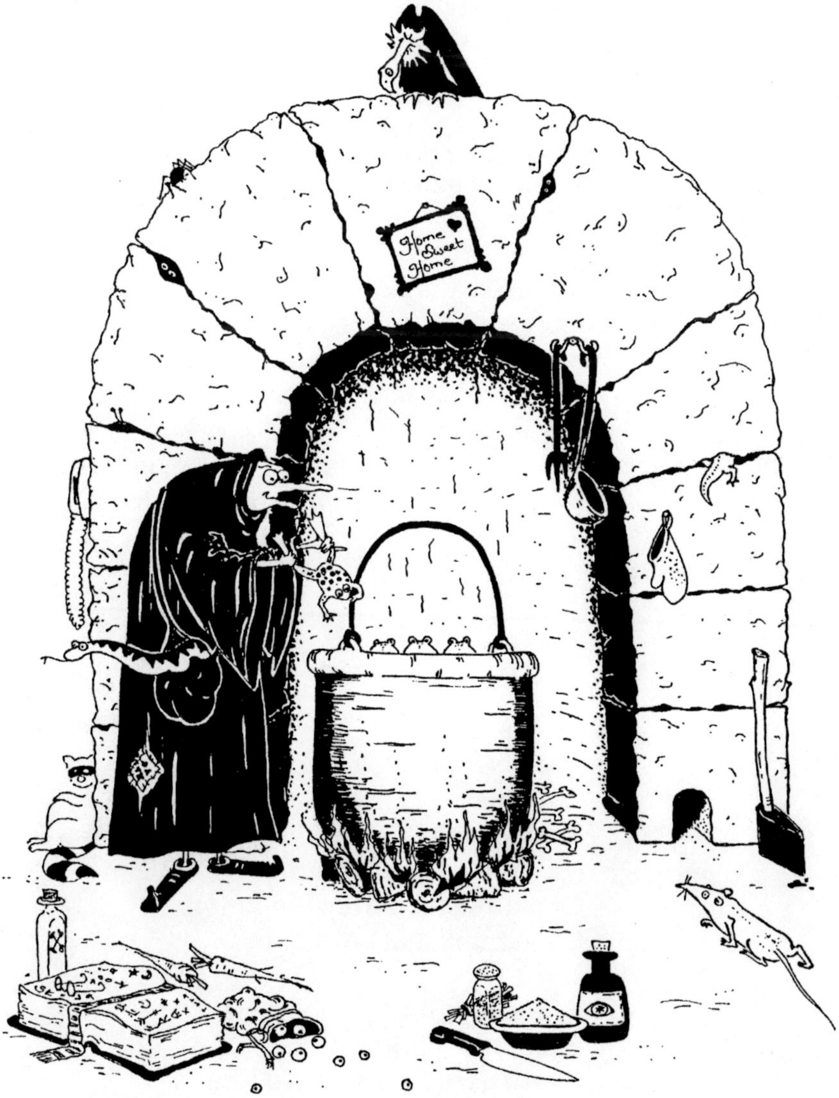
Home Sweet Home

There are also three syllable feet that have the emphasis on the first syllable, like the words:

calendar   **pri**or to

This kind of foot is called a ***Dactyl***.

So ***Dactyl*** feet have the emphasis on the first syllable. ***Amphibrach*** feet have the emphasis on the middle syllable. ***Anapest*** feet have the emphasis on the last syllable.

(***Dactyl*** is pronounced just like the end of "pterodactyl," with which I am sure you are familiar. ***Anapest*** is pronounced like "and a pest," without the "d." And ***Amphibrach*** is pronounced like "amphibious rack," without the "ious" in the middle.)

The next poem uses two syllable feet. The emphasis is on the second syllable. In the last line the word interesting works because it's pronounced:

in ¦ tri ¦ sting

Donut Holes

T **real**ly **likes** his **do**nuts.
He'll **eat** up **ev**ery **crumb**.
Of **course** he **leaves** the **holes**.
Don't **think** that **he** is **dumb**.

In**stead** he **threads** the **holes**,
Each **one**, upon a **string**.
See! **There** they **are**. He **hopes**
You **think** they're **in**ter**est**ing.

These two syllable feet are called *Iamb*. Do you hear the drumbeat on the bold type syllables? There are also two syllable feet with the emphasis on the first syllable called *Trochee*:

throw|ing   **run**|ning,

Do you hear the emphasis on **throw** and **run**? Do you feel the let down on ing? An *Iamb* has the emphasis on the second syllable. A *Trochee* has the emphasis on the first syllable.

(*Iamb* is pronounced like "I am" with a "b" at the end. *Trochee* is pronounced like "okay" with a "tr" in front.)

The names of the different types of feet are useful if you are talking about them, but you don't have to remember the names to use the pattern of feet that you want.

There are also names for lines with different numbers of feet. Again, the names make it easier to talk about them. That's all. These names are:

One-foot line	Monometer
Two-foot line	Dimeter
Three-foot line	Trimeter
Four-foot line	Tetrameter
Five-foot line	Pentameter
Six-foot line	Hexameter
Seven-foot line	Heptameter
Eight-foot line	Octameter

To summarize some typical lines you might use, a line of *iambic* trimeter, that is a line of three *iambs*, sounds like:

tiDUM tiDUM tiDUM

T **drinks** ¦ his **so**¦das **up**;

A line of three *Amphibrach* feet, sounds like:

tiDUMti tiDUMti tiDUMti

From **ware**house ¦ to **their** house ¦ by **ware**plane!

A line of three *Anapest* feet, sounds like:

titiDUM titiDUM titiDUM

The old **witch** ¦ in her **brew** ¦ dropped a **frog**

Dear T,

Yes, we can try to write a **limerick** or two ourselves. Lots of **limericks** start with, There once was a man from.... Why don't we start with There once was a boy from.... Let's pick the Indian city **Calcutta**. What rhymes with that? There are few, if any, true rhymes, but there are some pretty good near ones: "butter," "flutter," "udder," and "mother," if you change the spelling to "butta", flutta", "udda" and "mutta." What are we going to have our boy from Calcutta do? Suppose that we have him sit on something. Let's start.

The Boy from Calcutta

There once was a boy from Calcutta
Who sat on...

What?

...a sleeping cow's udda

What happens next? Well, if the "udda" is full of milk, it might come out.

The milk squirted out
Of each little spout,
Which he churned and turned into butta.

How do you like it? The last line:

Which he churned and turned into butta.

is pretty good because **churned** and **turned** rhyme with each other.

About *Internal Rhymes*

When two words in the middle of a line rhyme with each other, like churned and turned, it's called an *internal rhyme*. *Internal rhymes* have an effect similar to alliteration. They add humor, strength and melody to a line.

Do you think the last line of this **limerick** makes the poem funny? It creates a picture of a boy doing an ordinary thing. He's milking a cow and making butter with its milk. But he's doing it in a funny way: by sitting on its udder.

So now our **limerick** about a boy from Calcutta is nearly done.

About *Scansion*

The last step is to scan the lines or check the *scansion*. That means to check the lines to see if they have the right number and type of feet. We start by marking the syllables that are emphasized. We could underline them, mark them with Hi-Liter,

or put a little ´ over a syllable to show that it <u>is</u> emphasized.

A ˇ over a syllable means that it <u>is not</u> emphasized. Since we've been showing the emphasized syllables in bold type, we'll keep on doing that.

There once was ¦ a boy from ¦ Calcutta

This line is fine. It contains three *Amphibrachs*. (See page 62.)

Who sat on ¦ a sleeping ¦ cow's udda

As you can see, this line is all right, too.

How about the rest of the lines in the **limerick**?

> The **milk** ¦ squirted **out**
> Of **each** ¦ little **spout**,

These lines are both wrong. The first foot in each line is an *Iamb*. (Page 65.) We can fix it by adding syllables.

> The cow's **milk** ¦ squirted **out**
> Of **each** ¦ little pink **spout**,

This seems to work, except for the fact that these feet are all *Anapests*, not *Amphibrachs*. This is alright because there's a change in the poem at that point. The first two lines tell what the man was doing. The next two tell what happens because of it.

> Which he **churned** ¦ and **turned** ¦ into **but**ta.

In this last line the first foot is an *Anapest* and the rest are *amphibrachs*. Again we can fix it by adding a one syllable word.

> Which he **churned**, ¦ and it **turned** ¦ into **but**ter.

As you can see, the words churned and turned are each treated as just one syllable. That's because the "e" in each of the words is not pronounced.

So now our "Boy from Calcutta" **limerick** is finished. Here it is:

The Boy from Calcutta

There once was a boy from Calcutta
Who sat on a sleeping cow's udda.
The cow's milk squirted out
Of each little pink spout,
Which he churned, and it turned into butta.

Try singing it. It's singable. Do you think it is funny? Funniness (if there is such a word) is the test of a **limerick**. A poet named Ogden Nash, who was famous for funny poems, wrote a limerick about an "old man of Calcutta" who solved his snoring problem by wiping his tonsils with "butta". See if you can find it, and then compare them. We didn't do too badly, did we?

Dear T,

OK, let's try a couple of **limericks** about a man from Seattle. That's a city we both know and love. What rhymes with Seattle? How about "battle," "cattle," "prattle," "rattle," "tattle," and "that'll"? (Do you know the word "prattle"? It refers to silly talk that has no meaning.) We'll try "battle" and "prattle."

The Man from Seattle

There once was a man from Seattle
Who fought in a furious battle.
It went on day and night.
People died left and right,
But he lived lying perfectly flattle.

The Strange Man in Seattle

There lives a strange man in Seattle
Who hollers out nothing but prattle.
He yells out crazy things,
Flaps his arms just like wings,
And then takes a big swig from his bottle.

Do you think either of these **limericks** is funny? Which do you think is funnier? They're both a little sad. The first is sad because being in a battle is an awful thing. The second is sad because there are too many alcoholics and mentally ill people who don't get the help that they need. The poems make fun of the people described, the coward lying flat and the strange man yelling and flapping. **Limericks** often make fun of people. You have to think twice before doing that.

These two poems do have some good features. There's the alliteration of fought and furious in the second line of **The Man from Seattle**. (We talked about alliteration, similar first letter sounds, on page 52.) The internal rhyme big and swig in the last line of **The Strange Man in Seattle** is okay. The made up word flattle that rhymes with Seattle and battle is funny. The near rhyme bottle, with prattle and Seattle, is a weakness.

It's easy when you're writing limericks to get carried away with the rhythm and the rhymes. You also have to look at the big picture. That's what others are going to see.

✉ ✉ ✉

Dear T,

Compare the titles of the last two **limericks**. **The Strange Man in Seattle** is the best one. It tells more of what the poem is about. It compels attention.

About *Titles*

Unless a poem is extremely short, you should give it a *title*. It gives the reader an idea about the subject of the poem. If it is a good *title*, it will make the reader want to get into the poem.

There are different types of *titles*. Label *titles*, like **Sharing**, are very short. In one or two words they tell the subject of the poem, and that's all. Descriptive *titles*, like **The Strange Man in Seattle**, go into more detail. Suspense *titles*, like **Waiting for a Poem From Terrance** or **Do You Drink Up or Down?**, are intended to intrigue the reader. A good *title* gives the reader some idea about what to expect.

Here are some types of *titles* that you should not use:

1. *Titles* that run on into the first line of the poem.
2. The word "Untitled"
3. The name of the form of the poem, for example, "Limerick."
4. *Titles* that repeat the first or last line of the poem, unless that line is so strong or so different that repeating it adds strength to the poem.

Try this:

Go through all of the poems and try to rewrite the *titles*. Give the untitled haiku *titles*. See how many that you think you can improve or add.

Dear T,

The next poem is one your dad wrote, when he was about your age. It was published in the Honolulu Star-Bulletin newspaper and is included with their permission.

Bugged

by Matthew Dyer

If a praying mantis
Crawled upon my sleeve.
I'd laugh and say politely,
"Please, Bug, won't you leave."

"I'm sorry to interrupt you
and break in upon your prayer,
But your pokey legs and starey eyes
Give me such a scare."

About *Opening* and *Closing Lines*

This poem also shows the importance of good *opening* and *closing lines*. The first line of this poem calls up the image of a bug that most people have heard of but have not seen. The second emphasizes it by pointing out that the bug is not in some zoo, but right on the author's sleeve. The last couple of lines carry the image further. They describe the author's scare at the pokey legs and starey eyes.

Try this:

Pick one of these poems and decide whether the last line is as strong as the first.

75

Dear T,

The next poem is about an imaginary character. So that you know, a hypotenuse is the line from one corner to the opposite corner across the middle of a square or rectangle.

Try this:

Think up some strange, imaginary characters. What kind of weird things would they do? For example, there is a German book of poems for children called *Strewelpeter*. It was written by Heinrich Hoffman. It features, among others: Shock-headed Peter who never cuts his nails or combs his hair, Augustus who will not eat soup and so starves to death, Fidgety Philip who leans back too far in his chair at the dinner table, falls back and pulls the table cloth and everything on it on top of himself, and little Johnny Head-in-air, who doesn't look where he's going and falls in the river.

How about a character called Play-Ball Paul, a boy who misses out on life because all he will do is play ball? You could include all the different kinds of ball that he likes to play: foot..., base..., basket..., stick..., kick..., and all the others. You could tell all of the things that he wouldn't do. What becomes of him? Does he become a millionaire professional athlete? Add to your idea file the characters that you think up.

Hypotenusey Lucy

Hypotenusey Lucy is
   A girl who gets straight to the point.
She will not be deterred by a rock
   In her way or a nose out of joint.

When she goes out walking,
   She will climb over stiles;
She will march across fields
   Just to save a few miles.

Says she: "I go always
   From point A to point B.
I won't take the long way
   Around, via point C."

In talking, like walking,
   When shove comes to push,
She'll tackle the nettles
   And not beat 'round the bush.

When our Lucy is talking,
   She says just what she means:
"A circumlocution
   Is not worth two beans!"

Once she met a large lady
   Who had a new sweater,
And she said what she thought:
   "A brown horse would look better."

So watch out for Lucy,
   Who will stomp 'cross your lawn
And give it to you straight,
   Before she marches on.

Dear T,

Isn't it always the case that things end just when you're starting to have fun? You're Halloween poem is a very good story poem. The imaginary characters are great. The rhymes are fine, and the assonance (that is, when vowel sounds are the same) between **screaming** and **beat** is very effective. This is a major effort on your part and really good work.

A Bad Night for Trick or Treating

by T

On Halloween when I went out,
Everyone started walking about.
Then spooky spirits dripping with gore
Said to each other, "Let's play more!"
They tossed kids and candy around in the street
To the rhythm, the sound of a screaming beat.
All of a sudden a ghost came out,
And the spirits fled with a scream and a shout.
The ghost gave all the kids their candy,
And then he met a pretty ghoul named Sandy.
Sandy was little and really neat,
But all she had eaten was just one little sweet;
So the ghost said let's go for a trick or a treat.
And all the kids followed with happy feet,
Until the ghost and his little ghoul Sandy
Said, "Don't you think you've had enough candy?
Now it's time to say, 'Goodbye!'"
And all the kids began to cry.

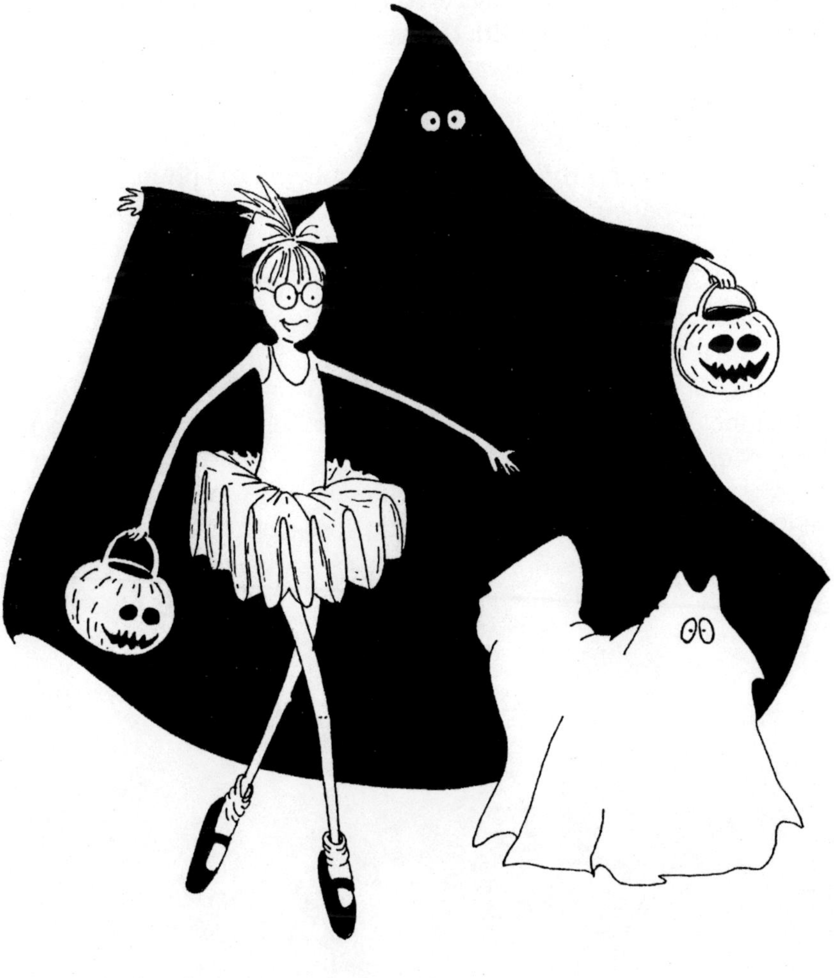

Dear T,

Your Halloween poem is a story poem. The next one is a nostalgia, or "I remember the way things used to be," poem. And it connects the way things used to be with the way they are now.

About *Point of View*

Another thing that's different about this poem is its point of view. It is in the first person. That means that in it "I" am doing the talking, but in this case the "I" is not the author of the poem. It sounds as though "I" is probably a woman who is the Mama's daughter and the kids' mother.

By using the point of view of a person other than the author, you can sometimes get very interesting poems. One of the best examples is *Journey of the Magi* by T. S. Elliot. In it one of the three wise men of the East that visited Jesus at his birth many years later tells the story of the visit. He explains the effect that Jesus' birth had on them. He tells it in the first person, "A cold coming we had of it..." It makes you feel that you're listening to someone who was really there.

Oops Oops Soup

My Mama was a darn good cook.
She always knew just what it took
To bake a cake or make a pie
That put a twinkle in her man's eye.

On her old stove she kept a pot
Of good, rich stock, all steaming hot,
And in that pot went lots of stuff,
Whatever there was that was more than enough;
She'd put in trimmings, bones and peelings,
And care and love and happy feelings.
She made mistakes: she'd overseason
Or overcook, or for some reason
Or other, every now and then,
She'd say, "Oops! Oops!" and scrape it in.
So "Oops Oops Soup" we called that pot
On her old stove, all steaming hot.
Because it always tasted good,
It was my favorite comfort food.
At night I'd say, "I'd love a bowl
To fill me up and soothe my soul."

Now on my stove I keep a pot
Of Oops Oops Soup, all steaming hot;
So when it's time for my kids' lunch,
And I must feed the hungry bunch,
I know just what to give my little troop:
Some nice, hot bowls of Oops Oops Soup.

A Game: *First Personning*

Here's a game that you can use to learn how to tell stories in the someone else's first person. Take a short rhyme, perhaps a nursery rhyme, that you know well, such as *Little Miss Muffet.* Think what she would say if she were telling you her story herself, in modern language. Don't you think that it might sound something like this.

> "Muffet's my name, Susan Muffet. I had this bowl of cottage cheese. (We used to call it "curds and whey," but now we call it "cottage cheese.") I wanted to eat it out under the shade of a tree. I sat down on a tuffet of grass and started to eat. At that moment a big, hairy, brown spider dropped down on the grass beside me. You could see the strand of web spin right out of him. Well, I certainly wasn't going share my nice cottage cheese with him, and I didn't want him crawling across my skirt; so I was out of there."

See how easy it is. And you might surprise yourself with some good material for a free verse poem. (We'll talk about them later.)

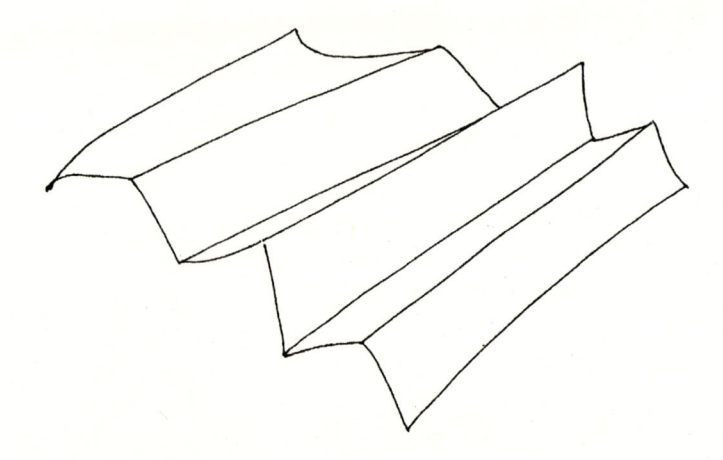

Dear T,

Another Game: *Exquisite Corpses*

Here's another poetry game for you that's really crazy. It's called *Exquisite Corpses*. What a name! Where did they get that one? Anyway it goes like this. You play it with one or more of your friends. Whoever goes first writes down the first line of a poem. He or she then folds it over, so that no one can see the line, and tells the next player what the next line needs to be:

> how many feet,
>
> what kind of feet, and
>
> what the rhyme sound is, if any.

The next player does his or her best to write the next line according to the instructions. Then he or she folds it over and tells the next player what to do. You keep on going until the every player has written one line or two, if there are only two or three players. Then unfold it and read it out loud. You ought to get really funny results.

✉ ✉ ✉

Dear T,

About *Poems in Special Shapes*

Shaped poems are not very common, but shaping adds an extra feature that's fun. The next is one that was written for a class taught by your Great Aunt Anne.

The form of the next poem is called a diamante. It is written in a diamond shape. It is supposed to represent a transition, something changing into something else, or a comparison of opposites.

You build a diamante like this:

First line:	A noun
Second line:	Two adjectives, describing it
Third line:	Three word telling what it's doing
Fourth line:	Four words making the change
Fifth line:	Three word telling what the last noun's doing
Sixth line:	Two adjectives, describing the last noun
Seventh line:	Another noun, opposite the first, or into which the first noun changed.

Catterpiggle

Catterpiggle,
Fuzzy, wiggly,
Crawling and gnawing,
Cocoon spinner, dream winner,
Struggling and flying,
Glittery, wingly:
Butterfliggle.

Here's another *shaped poem*. Really, the only purpose of the poem is to create the feeling of a full moon evening. (Watch out for moonburn!) Note that the poem has no rhymes, feet, or meter. It is *free* or *blank* verse. There's more about that later.

Milady Moon

Milady
Moon sheds
Sable velvet
Coverlet,

Steps carefully
    Down shadow's stair,
Then runs on
    Gilded toes
Over the raven
    Waves of a
Southern sea,
And lies
Moonbathing beside me on the silken, silver ribbon of the sand.

You can have good fun with *poems in special shapes.* You can pick any shape you want. Put your hand on a piece of paper and outline it with a pencil. Now fill in the hand with your ideas about what your hand, or your mom or dad's hand, means to you. Then erase the pencil lines, and you have a poem in the shape of a hand. Or you can draw an alligator and do the same thing. Just remember the things you say should be about the shape that the words will be in.

✉ ✉ ✉

Dear T,

About *Personification*

In addition to being a shaped poem, **Milady Moon** is also an example of *personification*. That means giving an inanimate object, like the moon, the characteristics of a person. You can do that in several ways:

> By calling the object a human name: **Milady Moon**
> By referring to it with a personal pronoun: **"she"**
> By giving it human actions: **sheds, steps, runs, lies down**
> By describing it with human adverbs and adjectives: **careful or carefully**
> By giving it human body parts: **toes**

Personification can add fun to writing a poem because it gives your imagination the freedom to explore all possibilities. At the same time, it can be pretty silly; so you have to be careful using it. You cannot rely just on what something looks like.

You can certainly use *personification* whenever there's truth to it. For example, you could describe a tree's roots as its toes clutching into the dirt for a drink of water. That's really what a plant's roots do. On the other hand, to describe a willow tree as hanging its head and crying with shame, just because it looked like that, would be a poor poem. What would a tree have to be ashamed of?

You can also use *personification* whenever it really relates to the person in the poem. There's a line in a song, "willow weep for me." It works because it really expresses the singer's sadness for herself. **Milady Moon** is better with her

> Moonbathing beside me on the...sand

than it would be with her alone, because the scene becomes the writer's perception. Be careful with *personification*. Using *personification* is like using a metaphor. You have to know why.

The next poem also uses *personification*, too much *personification*. It shows how you can make a poem funny by exaggeration. In this case it describes fairly accurately how a tree works, and how a tree's parts compare to a human's parts, but it overdoes it. It also shows how silly *personification* can make a poem.

About Sonnets

The poem is also an example of a **sonnet.** **Sonnets** are an old and formal type of poetry. They can be very beautiful. the **sonnets** written by William Shakespeareare are among the most beautiful poems ever written. This one is included as a challenge to you because of your wonderful Halloween poem. You can write a **sonnet**, if you try! Here's how **sonnets** work.

They are written in iambic pentameter. You remember that **Donut Holes** was written in iambs. And a pentameter line has five feet in it. So each line of a sonnet, in iambic pentameter, goes:

> tiDUM tiDUM tiDUM tiDUM tiDUM

A **sonnet** also has a rhyme pattern. In **limericks** the words at the end of the first, second and fifth lines rhymed with one another. The third and fourth lines also rhymed with each other. It was called an *a,a,b,b,a* pattern. In **sonnets** alternate lines rhyme, and then the last two rhyme:

first and third lines rhyme with each other
second and fourth lines rhyme with each other
fifth and seventh lines rhyme with each other
sixth and eighth lines rhyme with each other
ninth and eleventh lines rhyme with each other
tenth and twelfth lines rhyme with each other
thirteenth and fourteenth lines rhyme with each other

You'll see that it is an $a,b,a,b,c,d,c,d,e,f,e,f,g,g$ pattern. Finally, in addition to being rhymed with each other, the last two lines in a **sonnet** summarize or make a comment about the first twelve lines.

The Personnetification of A Tree

A tree's green leaves are not his eyes but fingers
And nose to breathe exhaust and grab the light
For meat and sweet as long as sunlight lingers
And then exhale in darkness of the night.
His toes are roots and shoots he sucks like straws
To drink up every drop that filters down -
He slurps and sucks without a single pause -
'Neath his big branching arms into the ground.
He also has one true inhuman part:
His perfect memory. For all to see
There's writ in rings between his skin and heart
All things that ever happened to the tree.
  If he were me, although a little sappier,
    Some past forgotten surely'd make him happier.

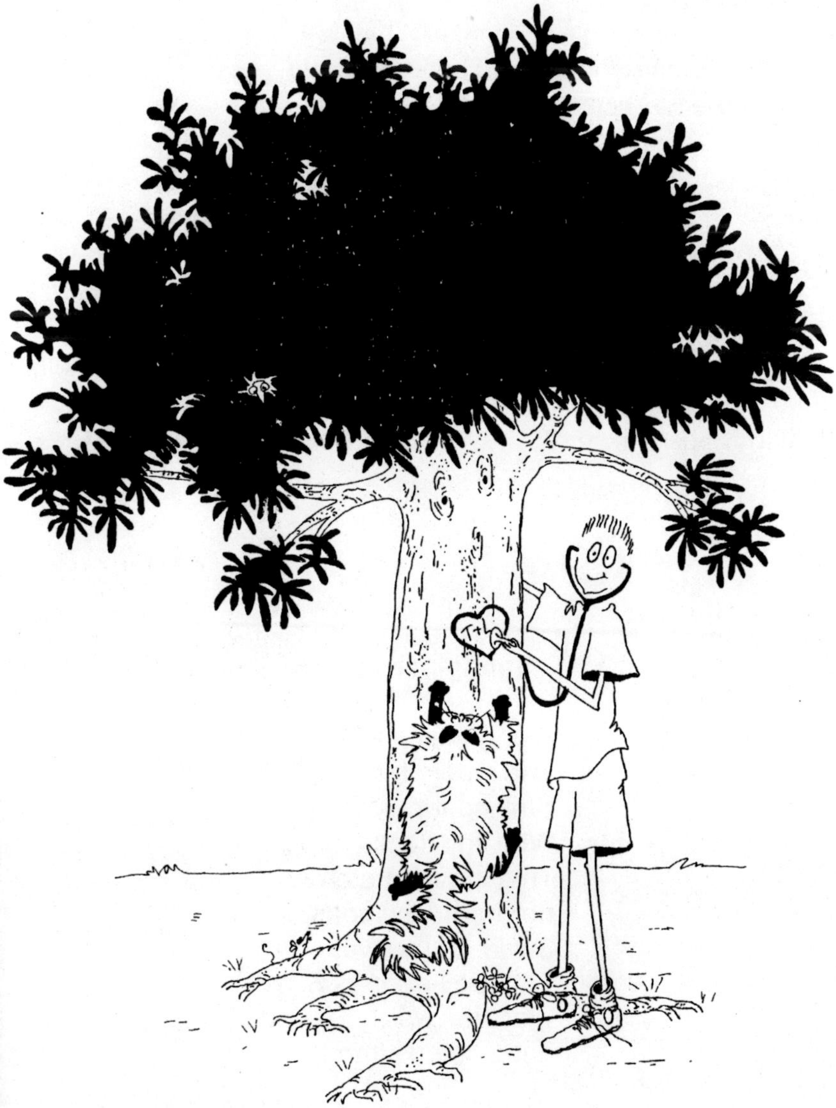

Dear T,

<u>About *Free Verse*</u>

The next poem is *free verse*. That is, it has no feet or meter or rhyme. We had *free verse* poems earlier:

> **Cats and Rats, Forever**
> **Star Light**
> all of the **haiku**
> **Milady Moon**

In writing *free verse* you have to be particularly sensitive to the sound of normal speech. The poem must sound natural. What do you think this poem means?

Sandpiper Tracks

Along the sand
The pipers run,
Striking the gold
With tiny tracks
That are no match
For barbaric floods,
Swart grey waves
The grey-eyed sky
Watches wear
The minted strand,
    Erasing,
      But not replacing.

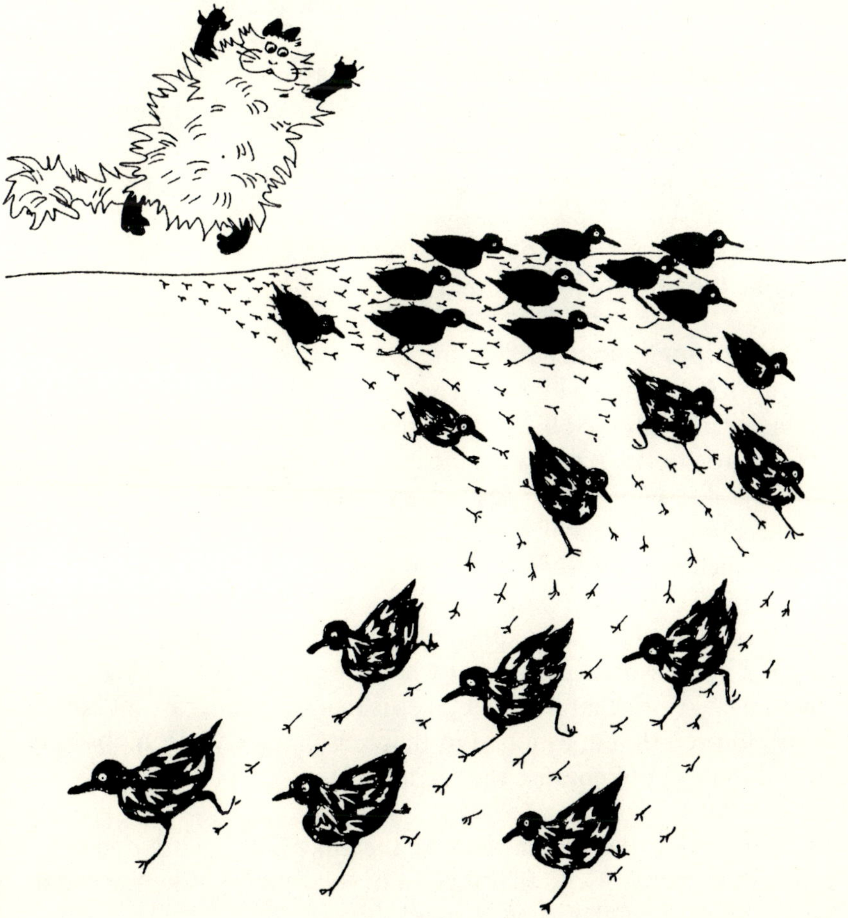

Dear T,

More about *Metaphors*

When we talked about *metaphors* earlier on page 25, we described them as comparing "things" with one another. In writing "things" are usually nouns, like "thunder," "short pants" and "asparagus."

Some of the best *metaphors*, however, are created with verbs. James Kilpatrick, who writes about writing, spoke of a woman who described a trio's singing as "braiding" their voices together. This beautiful comparison of singing with braiding hair or rope gives a feeling that the group's voices do not just blend in harmony. It suggests that from time to time one and then another voice stands out, like the top strand in a braid.

In **Sandpiper Tracks** striking the gold is a *metaphor* that compares the tiny sandpipers to kings and emperors who minted coins. The *metaphor* is reinforced by the later reference to the minted strand. (The word strand, by the way, means a stretch of sandy beach.) The barbaric floods of swart grey waves compares the waves to the hordes that overran many an empire in the past, leaving behind things, such as coins, that are just memories.

These *metaphors* are not explicit like our love is the sea. They are implied in the words and appear when the reader asks, "Why did he say that?" A risk that the poet takes is that the reader won't bother to ask himself that question. For that reason, don't be too obscure. You don't want to confuse the reader.

Did you notice that the waves erase the piper's tracks but don't replace the sand? Does that suggest to you that even the tiny sandpiper can make a mark that changes things? And even if the piper's mark is erased and forgotten, its changes are not undone. This poem is meant to give hope that even the least of us can make a difference.

A Game: *Getting More Out of Your Metaphor*

Here's a another poetry game for you. We can call it **_Getting More Out of Your Metaphor_**. You play it alone or with one or more of your friends. Start with a simple *metaphor*. It can be as simple as the ones that we talked about on page 25. For example:

> Love is a river

Of course, you can use "Life" instead of **Love**, or use anything else that you think a river exemplifies. Now add below the word "river" all of the things that you can think of that make up a river or relate to a river. If you're playing with friends, each player gets to add river things in turn. Remember to add verbs as well as nouns and adjectives. Your list might look like this.

Love is a river	Love is banks
flowing	fish
boats	flooding
islands	waves
wet	swimmers
sailors	shores
people	streams
rapids	shoals
water sports, all sorts	

Next, either by yourself or together with your friends, build a poem, relating to **Love**, or whatever other word you've used instead, all of the river things that you can.

Dear T,

Here are two more poems in *free verse*. The first could be about any sunny, winter Sunday in a Northern town that has had lots of snow. The second could be about a river that runs through any Northern town, after the first freeze.

For the Savor of Such a Moment

To explore the bare elms'
Crystal filigree against the blue,
He paused in crunching
Along the snow covered boards,
Between hip-high piles,
A frozen wave crest and trough beyond,
So white in the morning sun
That they turned his eye away.
The sound of the church bell
Cracked in the icy air, but
For the savor of such a moment
Prayers and sermons
   Had to wait.

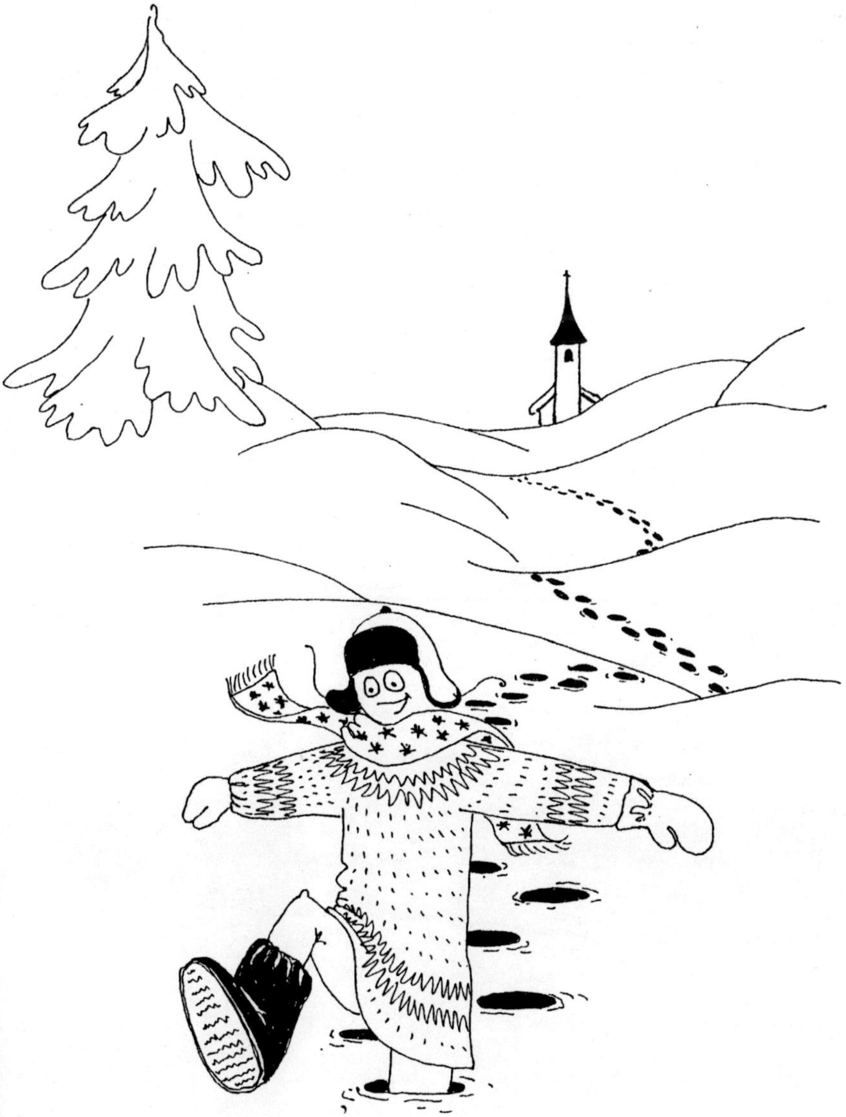

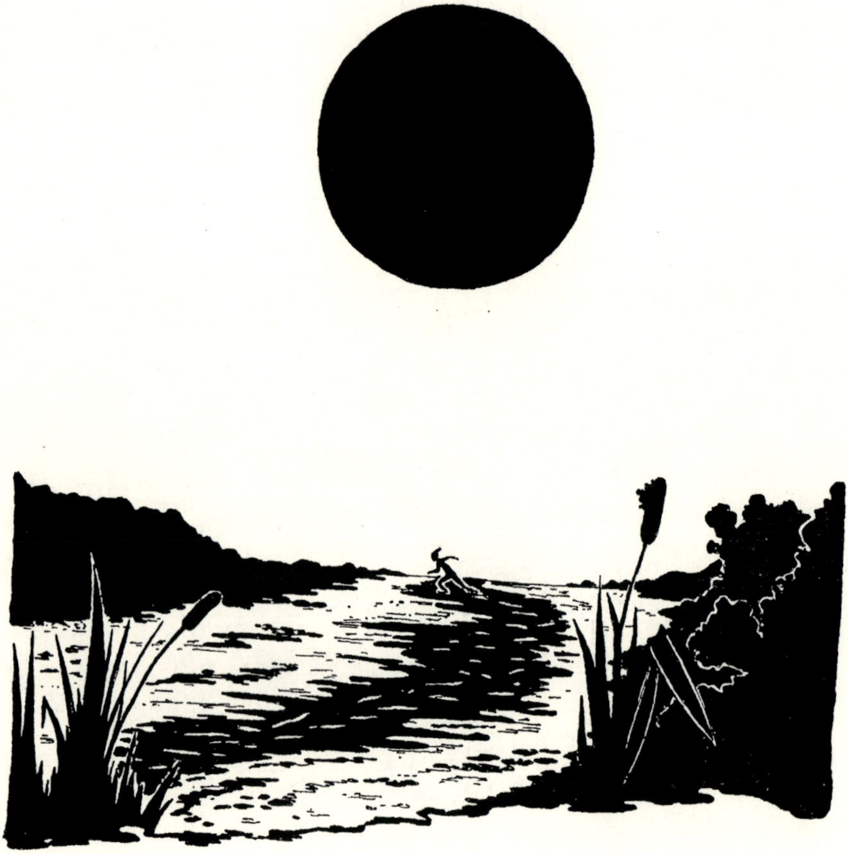

Black Ice

On the first fall morning
That the river ice is hard,
Clear and black, the world stops
For inspection by the skater,
Gliding silently, smoothly.
The river's banks hold
The town, the farms, at bay.
Beneath the ice are
Bubbles, trapped, black in black,
Leaves, and up the river,
As the way narrows and twists
Into the marsh,
Grasses, under and around,
And in the running, mirrorless black
The skater discovers, as well,...
                              The skater.

Dear T,

What do you see in your mind when you read these two poems?

About *Imagery*

These two poems create *imagery*. They each present a scene. The scenes are built in the details. In the first poem the details are: the ice, like crystal, on the branches, the snow covered boards, the hip-high piles of snow, the whiteness, and the affect of the icy air on the sound of the bell. In the second the details are: hard, clear black ice; a town and farms, bubbles, leaves and grasses beneath the ice, and a river that narrows and twists.

In the first poem the metaphors, comparing the icy branches to crystal filigree and the hip-high piles of snow to a wave and trough, add to the imagery. But even though these scenes are quiet, they are not snapshots. Time passes in them, when the church bell rings and while the skater glides up the river. This passage of time is the result of the use of the verbs, **cracked** and **gliding**. *Imagery* adds immensely to the richness of poems. Details, metaphors, and action verbs are the keys to *imagery*.

Try this:

Go to your journal or your idea file and pick out something important that happened to you. Write it out in simple, everyday language. Include all of the details that you can remember, or that you even think you remember. Then form it into a poem by putting the thoughts and the phrases into separate lines, one by one. Try to end the lines on strong words and important points. Then try to adjust them into a poetic form and language. Good luck!

Dear T,

Here's a last word of advice. We hope that you've enjoyed the pictures, the games and the poems. And think about the rest of the text. There are a lot of good ideas there. We hope that they bring you the joy of words and the fun of writing poetry.

Ever the best,

George & *Lena*

Advice

If you have something to tell 'em,
A poem in your cerebellum,
Scratch it on parchment or vellum,
And work on it 'til it's your best;
Then try it on friends for a test.
At least that's what we would suggest.

Dear T,

Just like the baker who gives you thirteen buns when you've ordered twelve (it's called a "baker's dozen"), I've an extra poem for you. You've asked for a poem about a boy "who had to go." Here it is.

George

The Puddle at the Table

A young boy asked his dad,
"May I please be excused?
I just have to go. Bad!"
But his father refused.
"No, you may not go, Lad,
'Til you ask correct**ly.**
It's your grammar that's bad.
You have to go bad**ly.**"
The boy answered sadly,
"Thanks for setting me straight.
I had to go badly,
But now it's too late."

WORDS YOU MIGHT NOT KNOW

adherents -	followers of a leader or political party
babble -	meaningless sounds or talk
boar -	a male pig
catacomb -	underground burial caverns
cathedral -	a large church
cerebellum -	part of the brain
circumlocution -	talk that evades the subject
codger -	a characterful old man
coven -	a group of witches
cranium -	the skull covering the brain
despair -	the complete loss of hope
deterred -	prevented from happening
digestible -	able to be thought about
diva -	the main woman singer in an opera
dotage -	feeblemindedness from old age
filigree -	gold or silver ornaments made of fine wires
galore -	many
grog -	liquor, usually rum and water
hypotenuse -	the side of a right triangle opposite the right angle
inflection -	changes in the tone or pitch of a voice

inhabitants -	people who live in a place
Jeroboam -	a large wine or Champagne bottle
metaphor -	an expression in which a description of one kind of thing or idea represents another one
mint -	to stamp money out of metal
nettles -	a plant with leaves covered with stinging fluid; an annoyance or aggravation
nog -	a drink made up of several ingredients
noggin -	a little cup, about half-size
nose out of joint -	this expression refers to someone who is upset or irritated
palate -	the roof of the mouth
parchment -	writing material made from sheep or goat skin
plights troth -	engagement to marriage
prattle -	meaningless talk, like a child's chatter
praying mantis -	an insect that holds its forelegs up in a praying position
puce -	a brownish purple color
pun -	word play based on words with similar sounds but different meanings
recluse -	a hermit, someone who lives away from others
savor -	enjoying a sensory experience
septum -	the center piece in one's nose
spindrift -	wind-blown sea spray

stiles - steps for climbing over a wall or fence

striking gold - stamping or minting a gold coin

swig - drinking a gulp

tome - a large book

torso - one's body, between the legs and the neck

trice - a short period of time, less than it took to read this

Tridents - U. S. Navy nuclear submarines

vellum - writing material made of fine grained skin

BIBLIOGRAPHY

Michael Bugeja, *The Art and Craft of Poetry*, Writer's Digest Books, Cinncinnati, OH 1994

Elizabeth McKim & Judith W. Steinbergh, *Beyond Words - Writing Poems With Children* (2d ed.), Talking Stone Press, Brookline, MA 1992 (contains an extensive bibiliography)

Richard Lederer, *Get Thee To a Punnery*, Wyrick & Co., Charleston, SC 1988

Clement Wood, *New World Unabridged Rhyming Dictionary*, William Collins + World Publishing Co., Inc., Cleveland, OH 1976

Shelley Tucker, *Writing Poetry*, GoodYearBooks, Glenview, IL 1992

Paul B. Janeczko, *How to Write Poetry*, Scholastic, Inc., New York, NY 1999

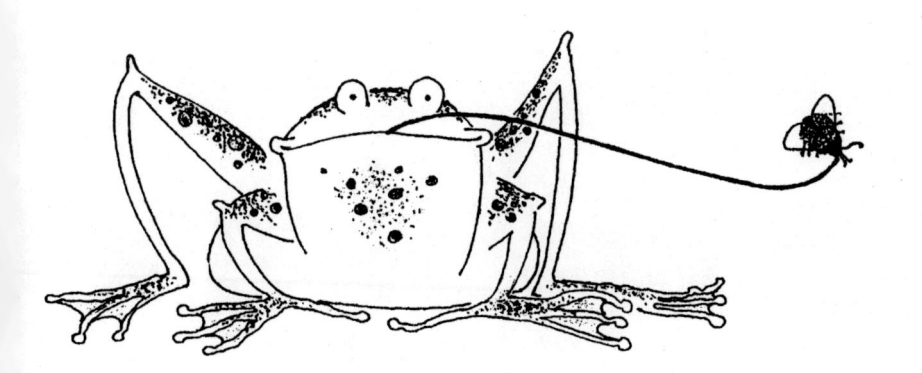

Idea Files

Idea Files

*Try **your** poetry here.*

9 781575 322872